THIS BOOK BELONGS TO:

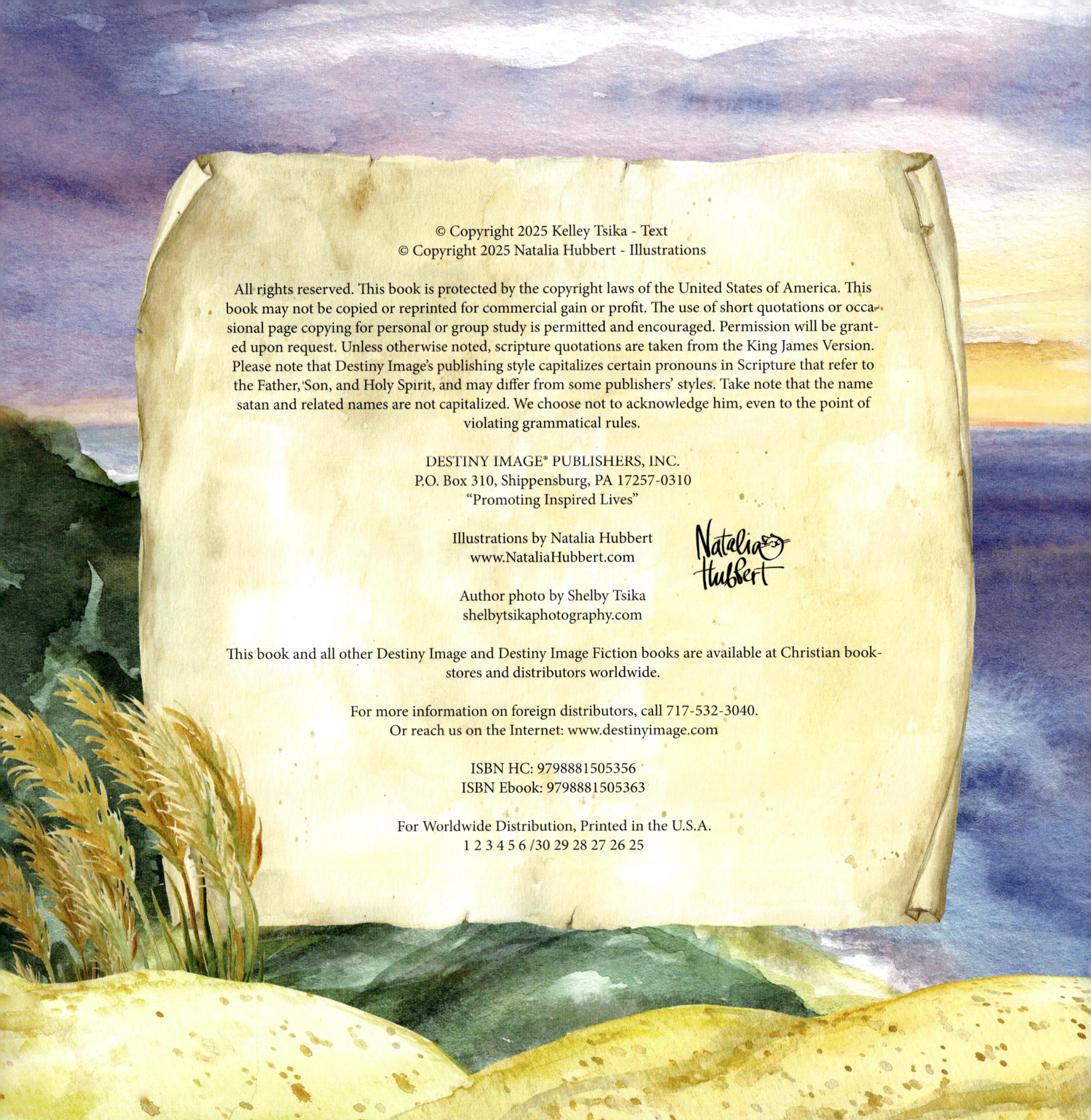

 Unless otherwise noted, scripture quotations are taken from the King James Version. Please note that Destiny Image's publishing style capitalizes certain pronouns in Scripture that refer to the Father, Son, and Holy Spirit, and may differ from some publishers' styles. Take note that the name satan and related names are not capitalized. We choose not to acknowledge him, even to the point of violating grammatical rules.

DESTINY IMAGE® PUBLISHERS, INC.
P.O. Box 310, Shippensburg, PA 17257-0310
"Promoting Inspired Lives"

Illustrations by Natalia Hubbert
www.NataliaHubbert.com

Author photo by Shelby Tsika
shelbytsikaphotography.com

This book and all other Destiny Image and Destiny Image Fiction books are available at Christian bookstores and distributors worldwide.

For more information on foreign distributors, call 717-532-3040.
Or reach us on the Internet: www.destinyimage.com

ISBN HC: 9798881505356
ISBN Ebook: 9798881505363

For Worldwide Distribution, Printed in the U.S.A.
1 2 3 4 5 6 /30 29 28 27 26 25

FROM THE AUTHOR

In our world there are messages of indifference, violence, lies, and hate. I wanted Lumi to write letters to your children to remind them Jesus loves them and He is always with them and when they have Jesus in their heart and life, His light shines through them to expel the darkness of today.

DEDICATION

To all of my precious grandchildren

To Paul and Billie Tsika, my gracious in-laws.
Without their generosity and encouragement,
Lumi would not be with us today.

TABLE OF CONTENTS:

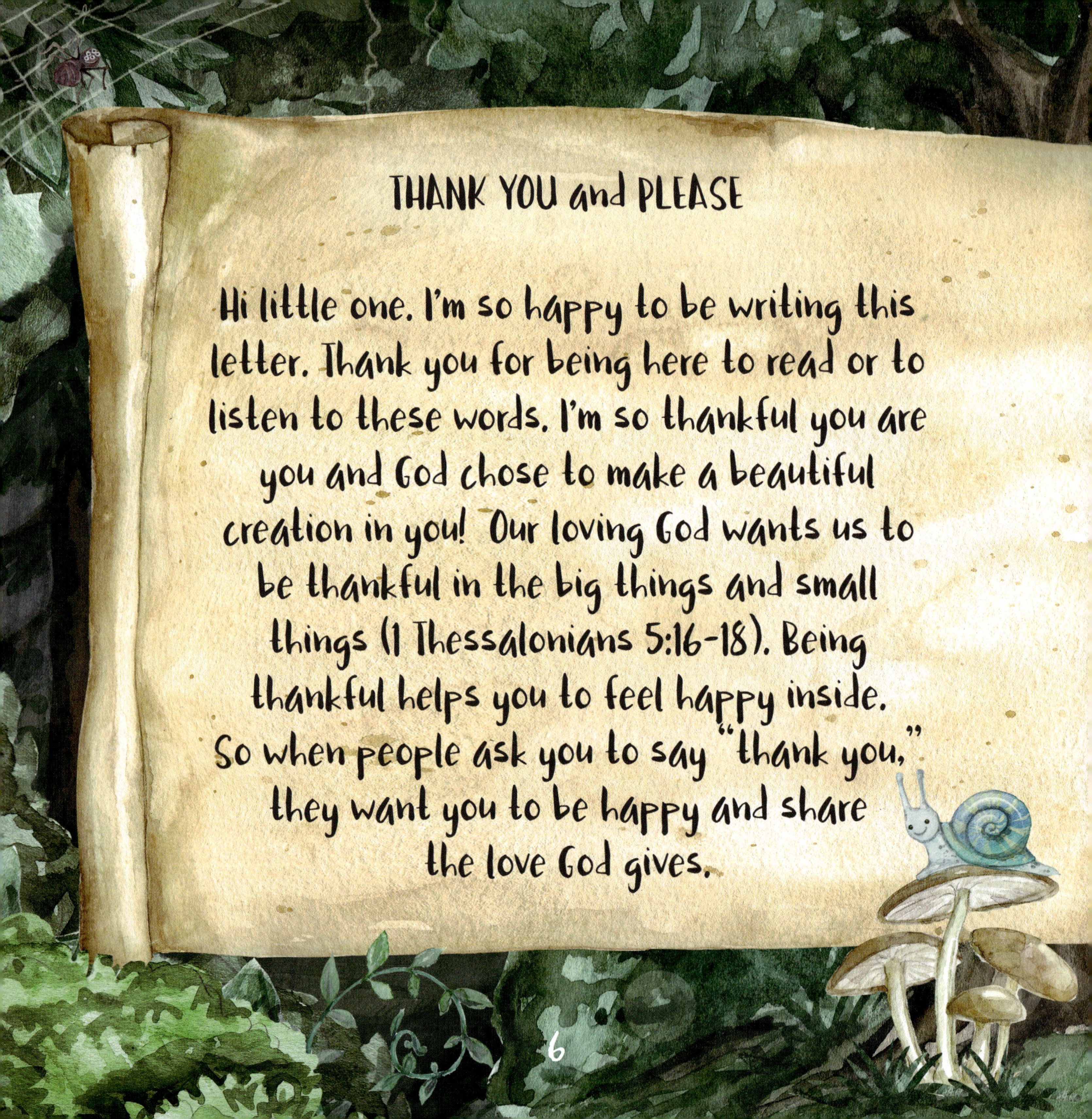

THANK YOU and PLEASE

Hi little one. I'm so happy to be writing this letter. Thank you for being here to read or to listen to these words. I'm so thankful you are you and God chose to make a beautiful creation in you! Our loving God wants us to be thankful in the big things and small things (1 Thessalonians 5:16-18). Being thankful helps you to feel happy inside. So when people ask you to say "thank you," they want you to be happy and share the love God gives.

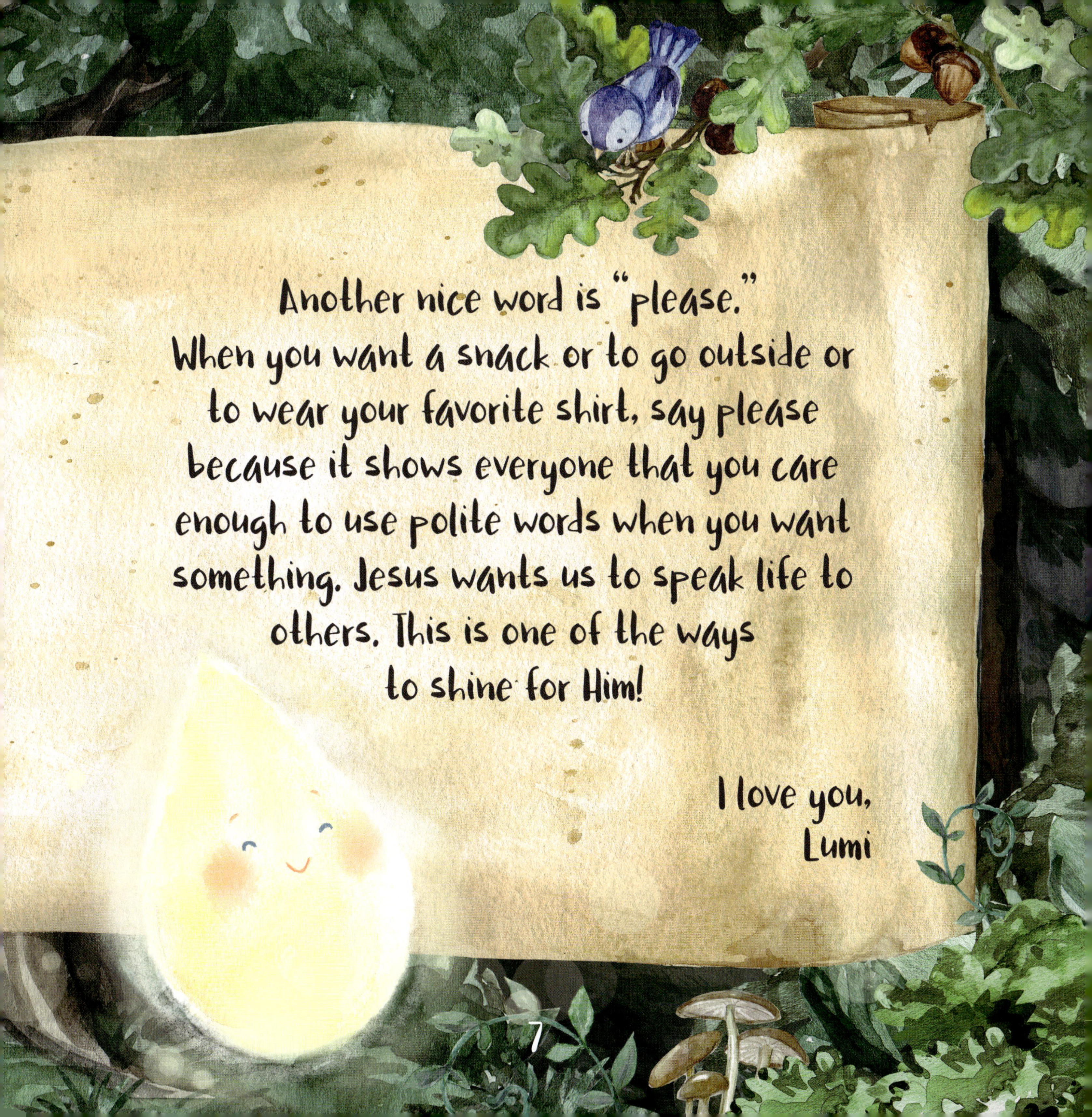

Another nice word is "please."
When you want a snack or to go outside or to wear your favorite shirt, say please because it shows everyone that you care enough to use polite words when you want something. Jesus wants us to speak life to others. This is one of the ways to shine for Him!

I love you,
Lumi

HONESTY

Hi little one. This letter is very important. It is about honesty. When you are asked about brushing your teeth or cleaning your room or about playing with your friends, God wants you to always tell the truth. Say what is true rather than what is called lying. For example, if someone asks you if you picked up your toys and you did not, then say you did not. I know sometimes it can be scary to tell the truth but it is always the best way to show love and to keep you happy (Proverbs 12:17).

Lying can sound better at the time but believe me, it is not! It hurts others and yourself and it is hard to make it better. Telling the truth in all things helps you to shine brighter for Jesus.

I love you,
Lumi

HELPFULNESS

Hello my friend.
I'm writing to you in this letter about helpfulness. God wants you to be ready to help someone who needs it all through your day. Your friend may need help carrying toys or may just need a hug, your teacher may need your help in the classroom, or your family may need your help with a brother or sister.

It is important to give help to other people around us (Luke 3:11, Acts 20:35). Also remember to ask for help when you need it. All of us need help sometimes and helping others helps us shine for Jesus.

I love you,
Lumi

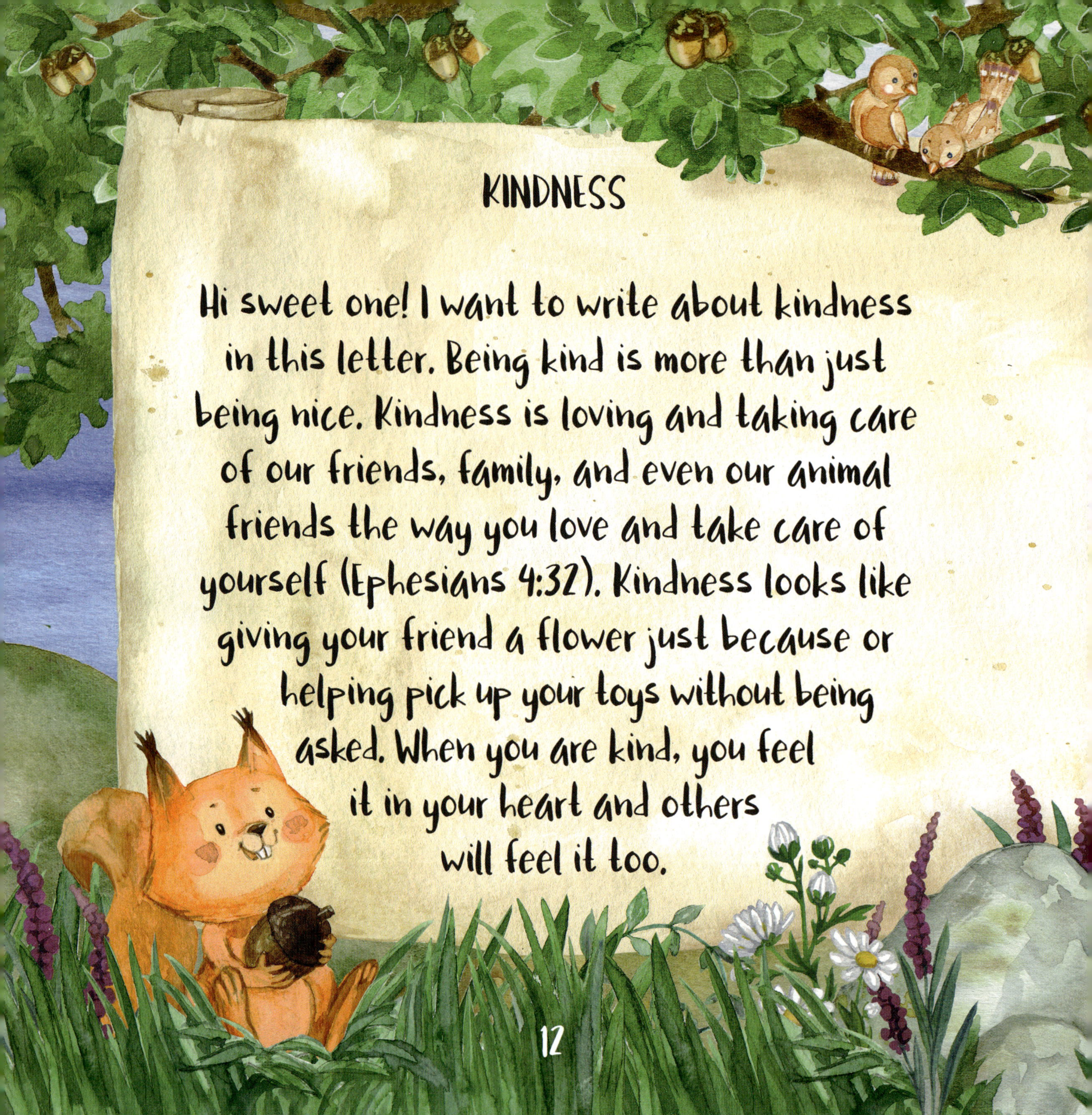

KINDNESS

Hi sweet one! I want to write about kindness in this letter. Being kind is more than just being nice. Kindness is loving and taking care of our friends, family, and even our animal friends the way you love and take care of yourself (Ephesians 4:32). Kindness looks like giving your friend a flower just because or helping pick up your toys without being asked. When you are kind, you feel it in your heart and others will feel it too.

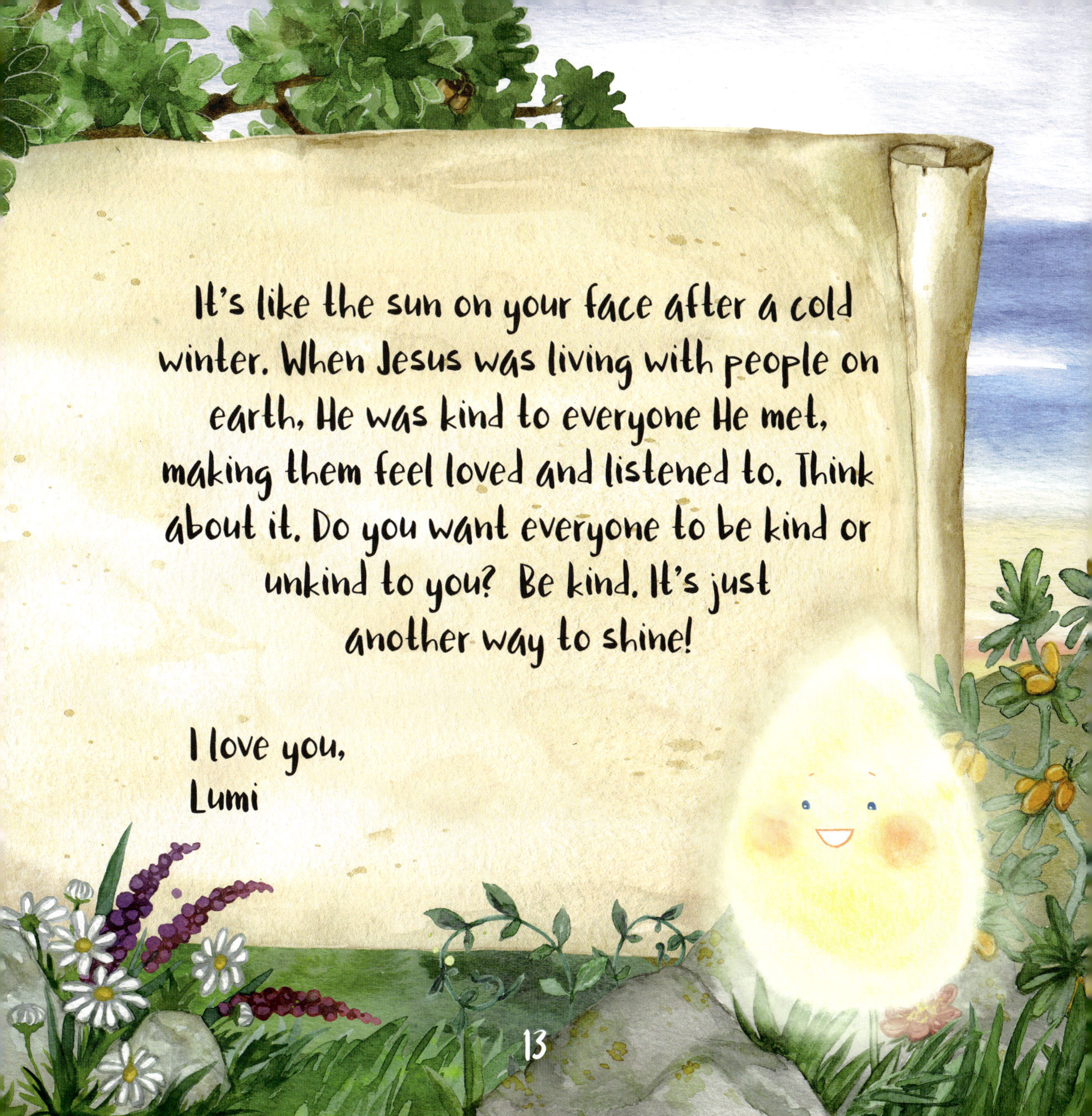

It's like the sun on your face after a cold winter. When Jesus was living with people on earth, He was kind to everyone He met, making them feel loved and listened to. Think about it. Do you want everyone to be kind or unkind to you? Be kind. It's just another way to shine!

I love you,
Lumi

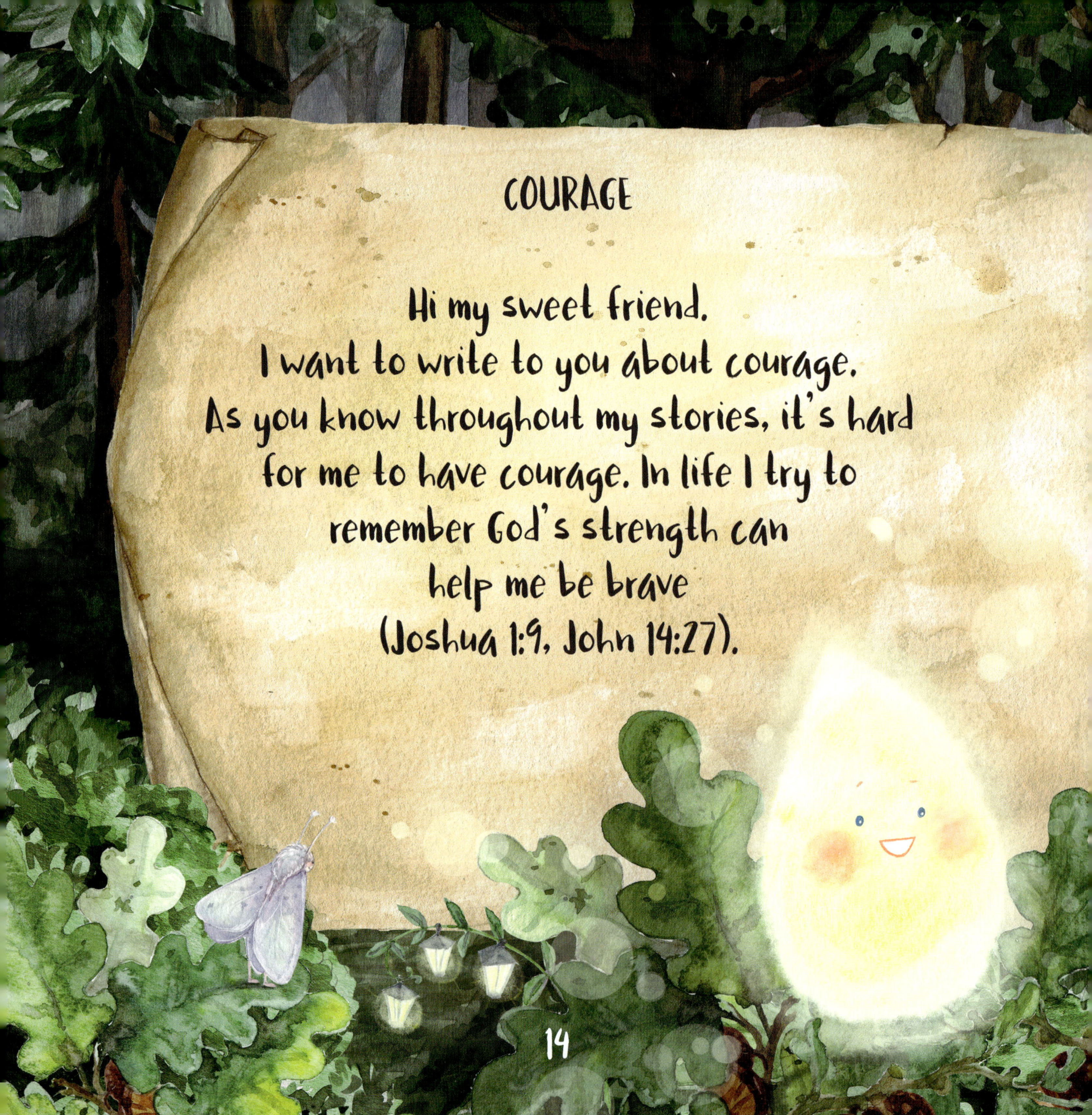

COURAGE

Hi my sweet friend.
I want to write to you about courage.
As you know throughout my stories, it's hard for me to have courage. In life I try to remember God's strength can help me be brave (Joshua 1:9, John 14:27).

When you want to try new things like riding a bike, swimming, making a new friend, or anything new to you, try to remember God is with you. Ask Him to help you to be brave! God's strength can help you be a light in your world.

I love you,
Lumi

PLAY/COMMUNITY

Hello love! I hope you are doing well. One of my favorite things to do is play with my friends. There are so many ways to play and have fun. These can be playing a sport or swimming together or playing a game, outside or inside. Whatever kind of play you like, the really fun thing about play is it helps you know your friends and family better.

This is called having a community, and when you have one, you are supported and loved during the fun times and the hard times. You laugh together, joke around, tell stories and just dream together. You are in a loving relationship, and good relationships are what Jesus wants for us (John 13:34-35)! Play together. Love and support each other. Shine for Jesus!

I love you,
Lumi

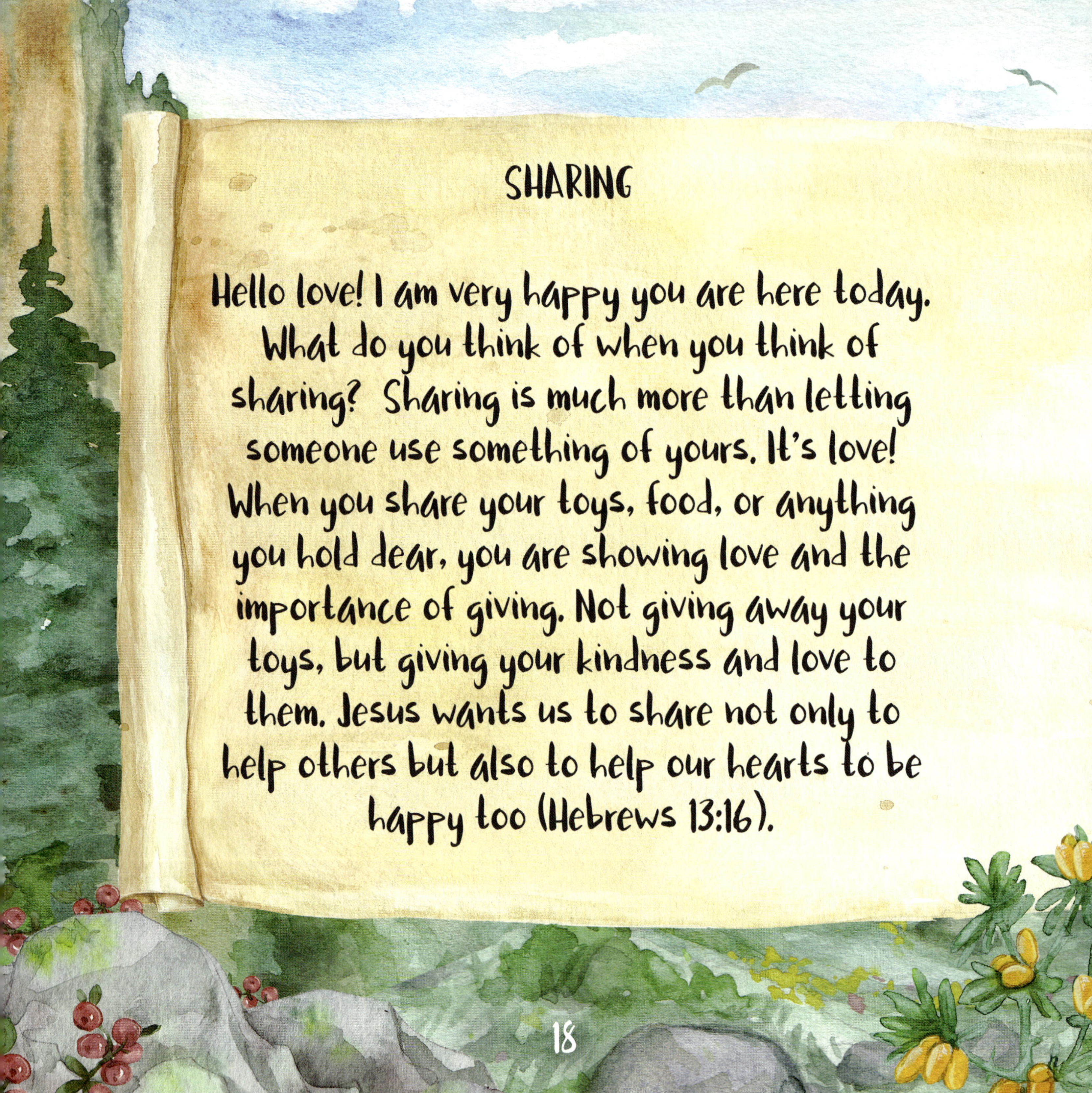

SHARING

Hello love! I am very happy you are here today. What do you think of when you think of sharing? Sharing is much more than letting someone use something of yours. It's love! When you share your toys, food, or anything you hold dear, you are showing love and the importance of giving. Not giving away your toys, but giving your kindness and love to them. Jesus wants us to share not only to help others but also to help our hearts to be happy too (Hebrews 13:16).

I know letting go of special things is hard, but letting someone play with something you love is ok and it will not be forever. The wonderful thing is that you will be a light and that makes Jesus so happy.
When you share your things, you are loving the person and that's the most important thing.

I love you,
Lumi

CLEANLINESS

Hi little one. It is so good to have you here with me. This letter is about being clean! I know you can get busy playing, being with friends and family, going to school, and helping around the house. In doing these things in life, you get dirty. It is important to keep clean. It helps you to be healthy and refreshes you to do all the things you love to do. Did you know God said our bodies are like temples, which are very special places to worship? (1 Corinthians 6:19).

We are to take care of our bodies like we would a temple! So the next time you are asked to take a bath, wash your hair and face, clean those little toes, and brush your teeth, do it with joy because you are taking care of your body for Jesus!

I love you,
Lumi

RESTING/STILLNESS/QUIET

Hi little one.
I hope this letter finds you restful.
I want to tell you about how important rest is. I know it's more fun to play, sing, run, and just be with your friends and family. Did you know God wants you to rest and be still too (Psalm 33:8, Psalm 46:10)? He made your body to have the strength it needs to move when you sleep at night.

It's also good for you to slow down and have some quiet time during the day. This is all good for you and helps you to do the fun things you love doing.
So rest up and shine for Jesus!

I love you,
Lumi

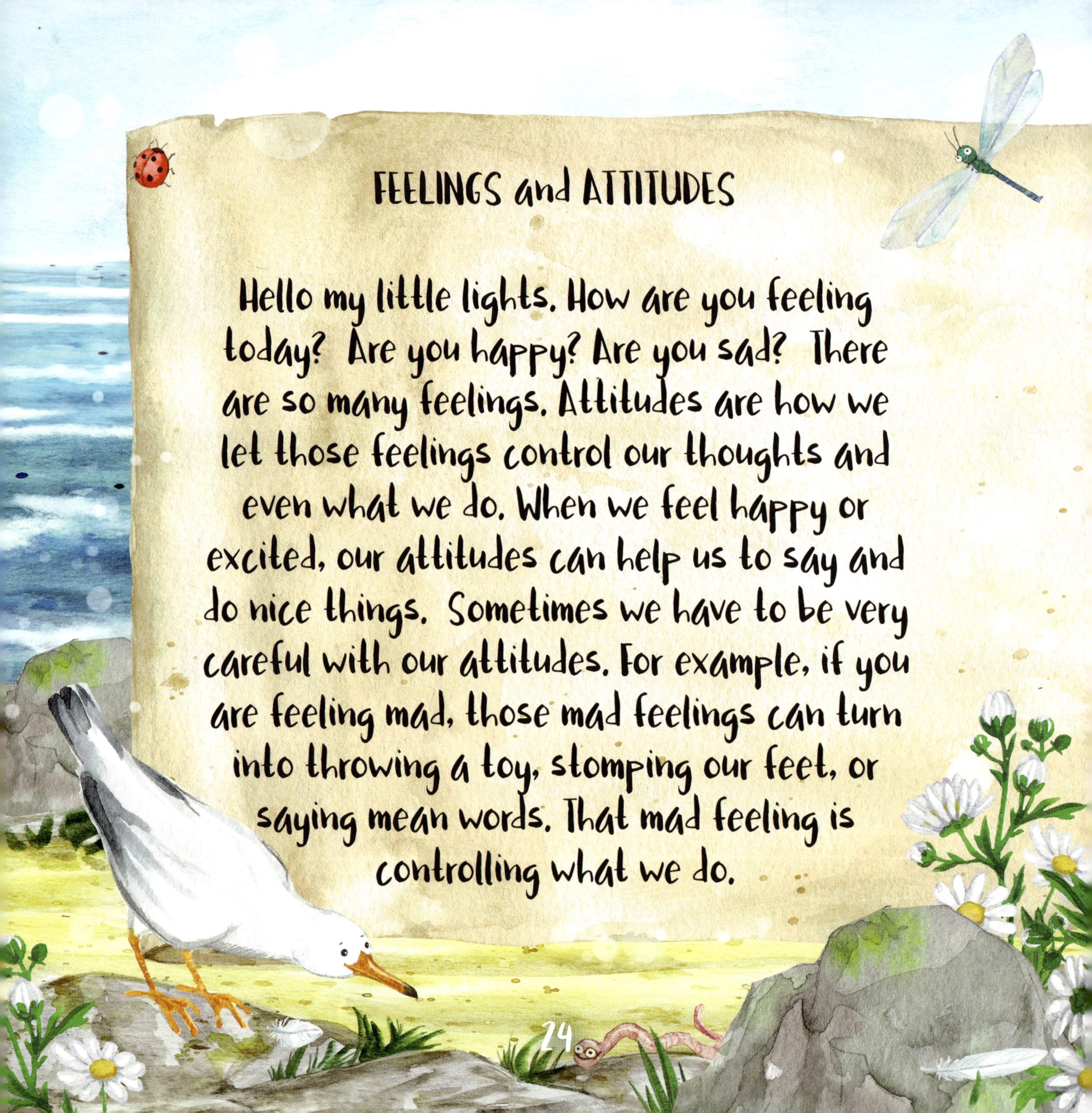

FEELINGS and ATTITUDES

Hello my little lights. How are you feeling today? Are you happy? Are you sad? There are so many feelings. Attitudes are how we let those feelings control our thoughts and even what we do. When we feel happy or excited, our attitudes can help us to say and do nice things. Sometimes we have to be very careful with our attitudes. For example, if you are feeling mad, those mad feelings can turn into throwing a toy, stomping our feet, or saying mean words. That mad feeling is controlling what we do.

Mad and sad feelings are okay as long as we don't hurt ourselves or other people and pets. In this world, you may feel happy, sad, mad, excited, and afraid. All of these feelings are okay. When Jesus lived on earth, He felt all of these and He leaned on His Father God to help Him with His feelings (Hebrews 4:15-16). If some feelings ever feel too big for you, please talk about your feelings with someone you love and trust to help you.

I love you,
Lumi

Hello dear ones.

Thank you for reading these words today! I'm so glad you're here. Respect is a kindness we give to those around us that have earned it. It is a consideration of feelings of the other person. It is good to honor and respect your parents and other caregivers. They take good care of you, love you, and help you be the person you should be. Listen to them. Let them help you in this life (Proverbs 19:20-21).

We all need help sometimes whether we are young or old! Think about how much they love you and only have the best in mind for you. This is respecting them. Respect those who are helping you along. It's another way we can show love and that lights up our world!

I love you,
Lumi

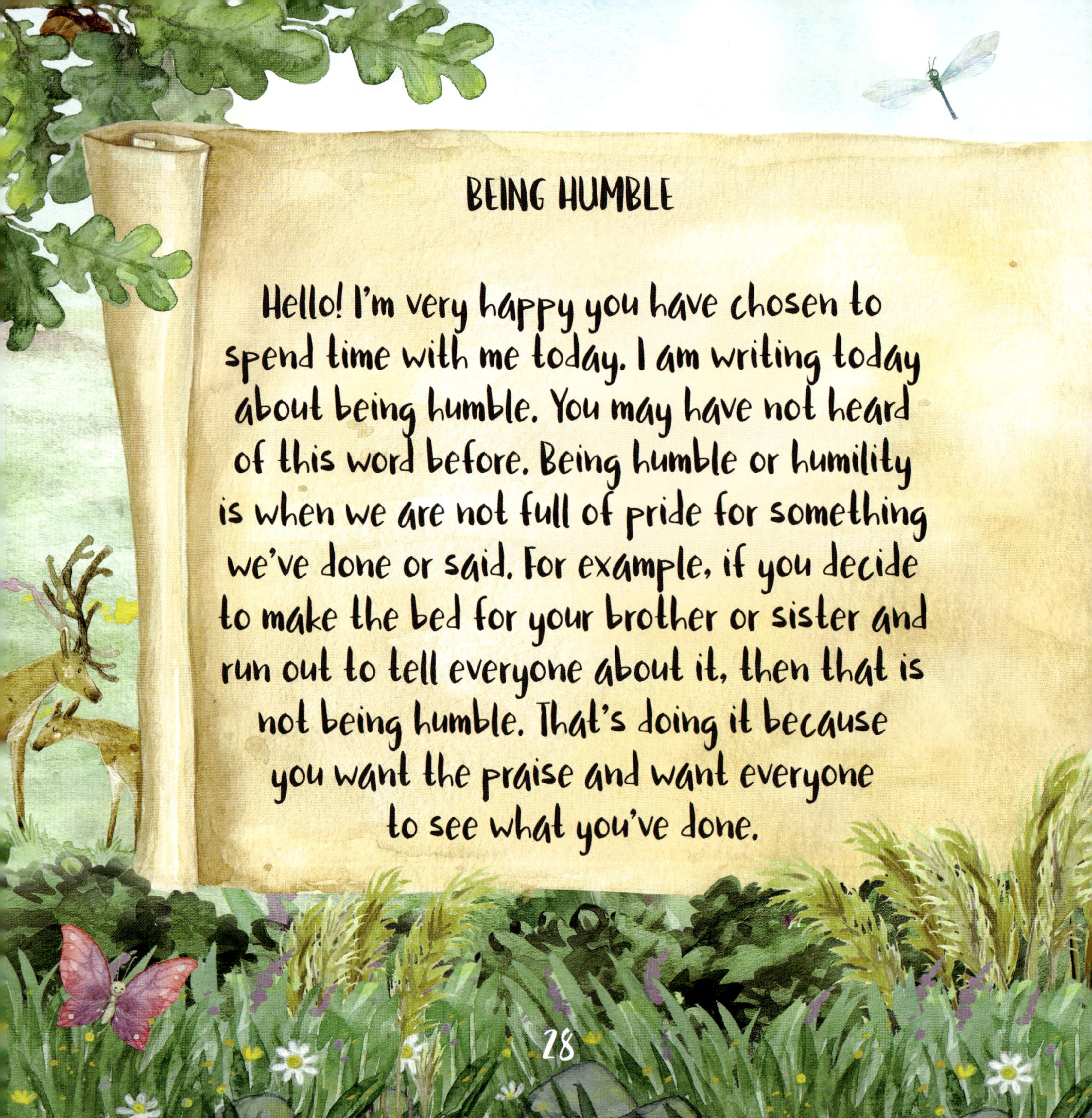

BEING HUMBLE

Hello! I'm very happy you have chosen to spend time with me today. I am writing today about being humble. You may have not heard of this word before. Being humble or humility is when we are not full of pride for something we've done or said. For example, if you decide to make the bed for your brother or sister and run out to tell everyone about it, then that is not being humble. That's doing it because you want the praise and want everyone to see what you've done.

If you do a kindness, try not to brag about it. The kindness will lose its value. When you are humble, remember God sees you and He is very pleased with you (Philippians 2:3). You are shining for Jesus and not for yourself!

I love you,
Lumi

LOSS

Hi sweet friend. I want to write about something that is hard and sad. It's about loss. You know when you have a favorite toy and you love this toy and play with it all the time? One day the toy is lost and it cannot be found. How do you feel about this? What do you do? Will you ever love the same way again? Now what if a special person or pet goes away? They are not lost. God knows where they are (1 John 3:20). When someone you love dies or goes away, it can hurt really bad and it's ok to be sad, cry, or even be angry.

Please try to remember God put them in your life as gifts of love. That's why it hurts when they are no longer here with you. You know what? When they go, that gift is still with you. The love never stops living through you. It was just their time to go. Try and remember the wonderful memories you have. Talk to God about your feelings. He will be with you always.

I love you,
Lumi

PAUL E. TSIKA MINISTRIES INC.
46 E Kitty Hawk St • Richmond, TX 77406
www.plowon.org • (833)999-9661
Write Your Own Letter to Lumi:
Send Lumi an Email at: Lumi@PlowOn.org
Or Find Her on Instagram: Lumi_the_light